Zoom... bang... boom

2

If you look up on a dark night
you might just see
a very funny sight,
a very funny sight indeed!

3

A bed!
A magic bed!
Gran's magic bed.
Gran's magic bed that can fly!

4

Gran's bed can fly.
It can fly high.
It can fly high in the sky.

5

Zoom, bang, boom
went the magic bed.
Up, up, up it went.
Higher and higher it went.

6

Over the trees
and over the gardens,
over the cars and over the houses,

over the hills and over the clouds
went the magic bed.

It got cold.
It got colder and colder and colder.

It got dark.
It got darker and darker and darker.

It got very, very cold and
it got very, very dark!

"We'll soon be where?
Where will we soon be?" said Jack.

It's fun on the moon.

Gran likes it on the moon.
Gran likes it on the moon
– a lot!

Jack likes it on the moon, too!

14